THE ART OF POSTAGE STAMPS

**Barbara Moore
and Honor Holland**

A WALKER GALLERY BOOK

Walker and Company
720 Fifth Avenue, New York, New York 10019

First published in the United States of America in 1979 by the Walker Publishing Company, Inc.

Published simultaneously in Canada by Beaverbooks, Limited, Pickering, Ontario.

Cloth   ISBN: 0-8027-0635-5
Paper   ISBN: 0-8027-7151-3

Library of Congress Catalog Card Number: 79-64893

Printed in Japan

10 9 8 7 6 5 4 3 2 1

PREFACE

This is a book of surprises, not only for the seasoned stamp collector, but also for all those who have never given stamps a second thought. For all, here is an invitation to enjoy some of the smallest wonders in the world.

In selecting stamps for this book we have been both painstaking and reckless. Many hours have been spent considering the almost one-quarter of a million postage stamps issued all over the globe since the mid-1800s. We have looked for the most beautiful stamps, taking "beauty" in its cross-cultural sense so that the intricacy of nineteenth-century stamp engraving competes with the symbolic brushstrokes of the East and the bold, graphic designs of the modern West. We have looked for stamps with stories—intriguing incidents and tales that often explain the how and why of individual stamps. And we have considered the extraordinary value of many postage stamps, including the rarest "classics" and some unique printing errors. For, while the value of a stamp depends largely on its being in top condition, philately is one of the few areas in which printing aberrations—those rare errors which escape post-office inspection—are highly prized.

In searching for the most beautiful, valuable, and interesting stamps in the world, we have sidestepped many philatelic conventions. The selection in this book incorporates stamps from every era and every part of the globe. The commonest, most worthless stamps are placed alongside the most valuable objects of a collector's dream when all that binds them is a comparable beauty. We hope that the pleasure of the unexpected will compensate the most rigorous collector, and that the unexpected beauty of the designs presented will attract the non-collector to the world of stamps.

All stamp values quoted are approximate at time of writing and are subject to wide fluctuations in the market.

"Turul carrying a messenger," an allegorical airmail stamp issued by Hungary in 1927.

INTRODUCTION

"Neither rain, nor snow, nor gloom of night stays these couriers from the swift completion of their appointed rounds." These vigorous words, inscribed into the stone of New York City's main post office in 1914, call to mind the romance traditionally associated with the mails. Links with distant or exotic countries, vital communications hurried through the night, news of forgotten or far-away friends—these are the sentiments evoked by the inscription and popularly associated with postage in the early part of this century. Then the valiant "courier" or mailman was still honored for his worth; the postage stamp, relatively young, was an ornate piece of design customarily depicting an illustrious series of heads of state.

The look of the postage stamp has altered radically since then, reflecting not only changes in the style of art and design but also an evolving social environment in which the concerns of the nation at large—its achievements and its setbacks—are given official expression. The modern stamp speaks of and for our majorities and our minorities; often its theme is international, reflecting the gradual drawing together of nations during our century.

But the stamp we use today is essentially the same stamp that we find in 1914, and even in 1840, when it was first introduced to the world by Britain. It is a mastery of contemporary design, incorporating in miniature format a vast amount of information, carrying national messages across the world in the form of visual images, honoring the heroes of its time, and capturing the imagination of thousands from many cultures.

The long history of the postage stamp begins hundreds of years ago, long before the evolution of writing. It begins with the powerful need of a people dispersed over the land to communicate important messages and information. In every civilization rulers and their governments have devised methods of proclaiming victories, conveying decrees, warning of revolution, and sending requests for help. At first, drums, smoke-signals, hand-signals, and shouts were relayed from one point to the next. Later, man himself, traveling vast and arduous distances, was the means by which these messages were sent.

Around 3500 B.C., the Incas in Peru established a communications system based on the *quipu,* or Peruvian knot record. The *quipu* consisted of a number of cords tied to a central cord and knotted at certain points. Both the colors of the cords and the position of the knots had particular meanings, which only the sender and the recipient could decipher.

Since the horse had not yet been re-introduced in Peru, the *quipu* was relayed on foot by couriers. The chroniclers relate that these runners or *chasqui* were capable of covering immense distances at such speed that they were sometimes entrusted with the delivery of fresh fish and fruit for the emperor. They were eagerly awaited at the relay posts since, although their *quipu* messages were supposed to be secret, they also carried verbal messages and communicated by their dress whether it was good news or bad that they carried.

Five thousand years ago the Sumerians developed the elements of the alphabet in pictographs—wedge-shaped symbols cut into clay. The clay tablets, once inscribed, were baked in the sun and then enveloped in an outer layer of clay, which was in turn baked. So, with the seeds of writing came the envelope, and for the first time man was able to ensure the privacy of his messages.

The question of privacy, or secrecy, remained important and led to many ingenious devices. Even after the development of writing—in the beginning a great art known to few people—the Greeks took the precaution of inscribing a message on the shaved skull of a slave messenger. As his hair grew the words were obscured, and at his destination it was only necessary to shave his head again in order to reveal the message.

In the fifth century B.C., the historian Herodotus, writing about communications in the Persian Empire, included in his description of the king's horseback messengers the phrase: ". . .will not be hindered from accomplishing . . . the distance which they have to go, either by snow, or rain, or heat, or by the darkness of night."

That two inscriptions as far apart in time as the 1914 New York post office building inscription and this one can be so similar, and yet relate to their own times, says a great deal for the advance of the communication system established by the Persians—a network of roads along which in 480 B.C. King Xerxes transmitted the news of his defeat by the Greeks at Salamis. Along these roads the couriers of the Persian Empire rode day and night, relaying their messages through a series of military posts positioned about a day's horse or camel ride apart.

Our modern word "post" probably derives from the Roman system, when mail was carried from military post to post. The Romans established the most efficient postal system of the ancient world, called the *Cursus Publicus*. Caesar had established a system of mounted messengers—a tradition adopted from the Persians. Emperor Augustus inherited this system, and turned it into a perfectly organized state courier service. Carriages were introduced into the service, and all along the

The hands of the stamp engraver and his tools—issued by Austria to publicize "The Day of the Stamp."

The "Quipu knot" on a modern stamp from Peru and a clay tablet from a set of stamps issued by Syria to show the development of ancient writing. (Collection, Viola Ilma)

straight, Roman roads specially constructed stations were manned by permanent garrisons of messengers, horsemen, and carriage drivers. Although the name *Cursus Publicus* implied that the system was for everyone, the use of this service was strictly confined to officialdom. Indeed, at first only the emperor himself, his sons, and certain high officials with special written authorization had use of it. The importance given by the Romans to their system can be judged from the fact that local villagers were officially obliged to supply the posts with food, horses, and fodder, and that the service as a whole was subordinated to the emperor's personal guard. In the nineteenth century the U.S. postal system was placed in the charge of statesmen such as Benjamin Franklin.

As literacy spread, more and more people began to take advantage of the various postal services in operation. Charlemagne, having conquered most of Europe by the early ninth century, based his system on the ancient Persian model and laid the foundations for the postal system of the Holy Roman Empire. In the Middle Ages, scholarship became increasingly important and a well-developed messenger service was created between the great abbeys and universities. The Venetians, as foremost world traders, established their own post routes and a complex system of envelope markings—our first indication of the postage stamps that were to follow. A pair of stirrups, for instance, indicated that the letter was to travel by mounted courier; *"cito, cito"* meant "haste, haste". In cases of extreme urgency a gallows was drawn, indicating the fate of the courier who neglected to transport the letter by the quickest means possible.

Marco Polo, himself a Venetian and a renowned explorer, described the wonders of the postal system used in thirteenth-century China under Kublai Khan. The Chinese system, which had been established two generations earlier by Genghis Khan, was reported to be superior even to the Romans'. Posting stations were dotted throughout the empire about thirty miles apart, even in uninhabited regions. Each station was a palatial hostelry with four hundred horses. Foot messengers wore bells attached to their belts, so that the next messenger would hear their approach and prepare to take over. These relay foot messengers aided the mounted couriers at night by running in front of them with lanterns. Like the Venetians, the Chinese "stamped" their envelopes—a sun and moon, for instance, meaning that the letter had to travel day and night. And, as in other early postal systems, messengers were under threat of death if their entrusted communications were not delivered on time.

But the Chinese system, like so many early services, was

not available to the general public. The first true mail system for the common man was established by the Italian family of Della Torre e Tasso, which over a period of four hundred years succeeded in monopolizing the mails of Europe and acquiring vast wealth and influence as a result. The family—whose name was later Germanized to von Thurn und Taxis—began with a service for the delivery of letters in their native northern Italy. Later, one of them was appointed postmaster to Frederick III, Holy Roman Emperor in Germany, where a postal service was organized for the imperial possessions in Europe. The family's success was founded on their recognition of the need for an efficient postal system to be used by the many rulers of Europe, which was still divided into an unruly number of principalities. The Thurn und Taxis network, based in Belgium, eventually covered the whole of Europe except England and France, extending through the Netherlands, Spain, Italy, Germany, and Austria. It was not until 1867 that the last Thurn und Taxis postal service was taken over by the Kingdom of Prussia.

The Thurn und Taxis network was not the only system operating in Europe. From the Middle Ages onward France had its own service—the most extensive in its time—and it was in England, where by 1637 a national service was in existence, that some of the most important postal improvements were made. Instead of implementing a fixed fee, the English introduced charges based on weight and distance carried. In 1661, a man named Henry Bishop introduced the first postmark. It was a circular hand-stamp showing the date of mailing—a simple but important idea that deterred the customary delay of the mail. The hand-stamp remained in use in Britain, the American colonies, and India until 1787.

By the early nineteenth century postage had become very expensive, and beyond the means of many people. The postal authorities found it increasingly difficult to implement their system. The main problem lay in the fact that it was the recipient of the letter who was responsible for the payment of postage. Many letters were refused on delivery, either because of an inability to pay, or because the sender had craftily employed one of several devices invented by the public to avoid payment. An envelope could easily be marked with a coded message or symbol so that without accepting and opening the letter its recipient was able to tell that "all is well" or "come soon." This became a fine and much practiced art, especially in Britain.

Finally, in 1837, an English schoolmaster by the name of Rowland Hill devised a means of avoiding these problems and ensuring an efficient and affordable postal service. He ex-

Two sixteenth-century letter carriers on Austrian stamps. *(Collection, Viola Ilma)*

(Above) The first postmistress, Countess von Thurn und Taxis, depicted on a modern stamp by Belgium to mark "The Day of the Stamp." *(Collection, Viola Ilma)*

None of the entries submitted to the Treasury stamp competition was accepted by the "father" of modern postage, Rowland Hill. But a medal *(right)* struck in 1837 and engraved by William Wyon, chief engraver at the Royal Mint, provided the basis for Henry Corbould's watercolor sketch of Queen Victoria. *(By courtesy of the British Post Office)*

plained his ideas in a pamphlet entitled "Post Office Reform: Its Importance and Practicability." Hill proposed the prepayment of postage and a uniform rate of charges. Payment would be indicated by a postage stamp attached to the envelope. These suggestions were at first vigorously opposed by the postmaster general and by many influential people in Parliament and the House of Lords. The pamphlet was ridiculed. Some thought it would bankrupt the post office; others said that the notion of prepayment was an insult to the recipient. But within two years Rowland Hill had managed to overcome these obstacles, and he was told to proceed with his plans.

The first step in Hill's postal reform was to find a suitable design for the postage stamp. A competition was arranged, attracting nearly three thousand entries. But the final choice was a design by a non-contestant, Henry Corbould, adapted from a medal by William Wyon depicting the young Queen Victoria. Perkins, Bacon and Petch, the London firm headed by Jacob Perkins, the former printer of inimitable bank notes in New England, was chosen to print the first-ever postage stamps—the Penny Black and the Twopenny Blue of 1840.

(Left) Two Whiting essays, well-known examples from the many stamp designs rejected by Rowland Hill. Recognizing the risk of forgery involved in this form of prepaid postage, Whiting incorporated in his stamp designs the intricate machine tooling used as a security device in the printing of bank notes.

The sketch was reduced to a line drawing which, once engraved, seemed to Hill a suitable design for the world's first stamp. And so the Penny Black *(center)* came into being in May 1840, followed by the Twopenny Blue *(below)*. These were the final result of a long process in which a combination of several contemporary talents succeeded in defining the look of the postage stamp.

An unused single copy of the Penny Black from "Plate VII" recently sold at auction for $3,600. The Twopenny Blue, acclaimed as one of the world's finest stamps, is worth about four times that much. *(All stamps this page from the National Postal Museum, Philips Collection, London)*

FIRSTS—WHERE IT ALL BEGAN

Gradually a few isolated countries and principalities followed Great Britain's firsts—the Penny Black and Twopenny Blue of 1840—with their own stamps for the prepayment of postage. It was a slow process. Between 1840 and 1850 only six other countries issued stamps: Brazil in 1843; Switzerland in 1843; the United States issued two stamps in 1847; and in 1849 Belgium, France, and Bavaria followed suit. The seven countries set the scene for a worldwide postal system. By 1880 about seventy-five more countries were issuing stamps, and an organization known as the Universal Postal Union had been established in 1874 to regulate the traffic of mail from one country to another and to fix a scale of postage rates. This marked the beginning of an era of international postal agreements.

Since then the world map has changed considerably. Many countries and stamp-issuing entities have disappeared and a host of new nations has emerged. One of the first responsibilities for a new country is to define and publicize itself by issuing its own postage stamps. Since the firsts of the mid-nineteenth century almost one-quarter of a million stamps have been designed. Some have been printed two or three million times—and the United States has been known to print three-and-a-half billion copies of one stamp design alone. But only a few of these stamps have achieved the fame and value of the world's firsts, which now command prices in the thousands of dollars.

(Right) **Brazil's second stamp, of 1844, developed from the "Bull's Eye" design of her first issue and** *(above)* **the famous "Zurich 4" of 1843, Switzerland's first stamp which may now fetch about $13,000 a single copy.** *(Photo courtesy Friedl Expert Committee, New York)*

U.S.A. firsts *(below).* The United States was the fourth country to issue adhesive stamps. Since living persons are not customarily depicted on American stamps, Benjamin Franklin *(left)* and George Washington *(right)* were chosen for the 1847 United States firsts. Benjamin Franklin had been postmaster of North America (including Canada) prior to the American Revolution. The picture used for the stamp probably came from an engraving first made for use on bank notes. The design for the Washington stamp was derived from a famous portrait by Gilbert Stuart. *(Reference collection, Philatelic Foundation, New York)*

In Switzerland, until 1850, individual towns issued their own stamps for local and national use. One stamp carried a letter to local destinations, two transported it beyond the city limits. Basel was the third such Swiss town to issue stamps, with the beautiful "Basel Dove" of 1845. This rare block of fifteen stamps *(right)* has become a priceless museum piece, while a single copy may be worth up to $10,000. *(Photo courtesy PTT, Switzerland) (Facing page)* More firsts: from the Kingdom of Bavaria—issued in 1849-1858 *(below, left)* and 1862 *(above, right)*; from India, in 1854 *(above, left)*; from Peru, whose first of 1850 joined the new wave of stamps to be issued in the subsequent twenty years *(below, right);* and from Uruguay, whose delicate first of 1856 *(center)* is known as "El Sol de Mayo"—the sun's head emanating a hundred and five rays, and inscribed "diligence." The example shown is in fact a near-perfect forgery by the famous French forger, Fournier.

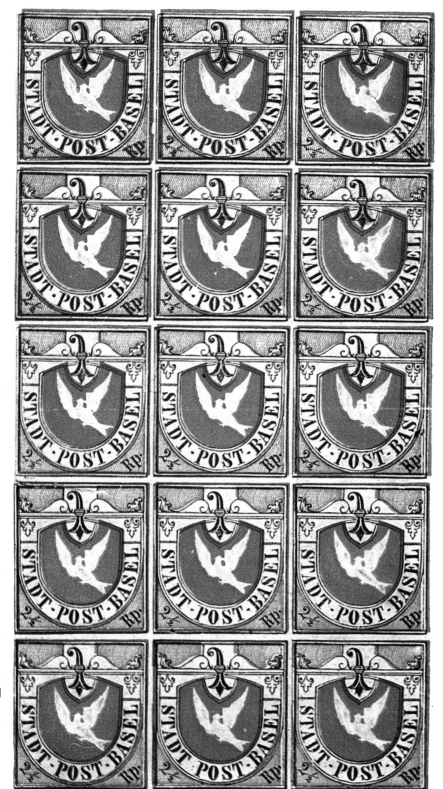

Romania's first of 1858 *(above, right)*—a hand-printed stamp—and the Finnish coat of arms above entwined post horns on Finland's first of 1856 *(above, left)*. The intricate first from Japan *(center)*, issued in 1872, shows two dragons, tails entwined, the Japanese heraldic symbol.

"Hope seated" is depicted on the first stamp from the Cape of Good Hope, issued in 1853 *(below)*.

(Facing page) France's first of 1849 *(above, right)* with Ceres' head calling forth wealth and bounty; Tuscany *(above, left)*, in 1851 an independent kingdom in what is now known as Italy but once under French rule, expresses this heritage on its first which shows a lion from the statue by Donatello holding a shield which bears the French fleur-de-lys; Nova Scotia *(below, left)*, which was a British crown colony at the time of her first in 1851, with an intricate design bearing the heraldic emblems of the British Empire—rose, shamrock, thistle and daffodil; and Barbados *(below, right)* which under British rule portrays Britannia on the first issue of 1852. *(Reference collection, Philatelic Foundation, New York)*

A MEANS OF REMEMBERING

Every year hundreds of "commemorative" stamps are issued, stamps for special occasions, special personalities, special achievements. Centenaries of the births and deaths of important artists, statesmen, and national heroes are marked. Accomplishments in science, sports, and world affairs are recorded or recalled. Major expositions or events find their way onto stamps. In this way nations publicize their successes large and small, adulate their heroes, and pay tribute to achievement on an international scale.

Commemorative issues are also a means by which countries can collect revenue to fund expensive occasions. Some nations even issue commemorative stamps for events in which they have played no part, tempting the stamp-buying public with bright, narrative designs. But, however valid a particular stamp issue might be, commemoratives of every kind are a fascinating reflection of the official spotlight on public events and personalities in any one country.

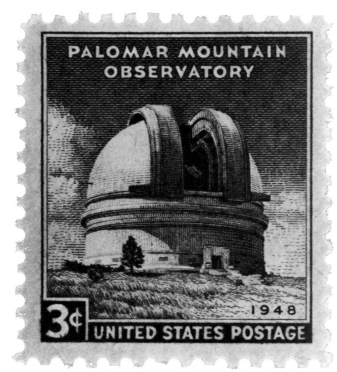

The Spirit of '76 *(facing page).* **The United States Bicentennial of 1976 captured the world's attention. Although many countries issued stamps for the occasion, the United States commemoratives were the most lively celebrations and featured some legendary scenes. The "Boston Tea Party"** *(above)* **was issued in 1973 for its bicentenary and the famous fife and drum "Spirit of 76," after a painting by Archibald Willard, was issued in 1976. Both are depicted with a composite block or strip of stamps—a device frequently used.**

The United States stamp *(left)* **was issued in 1948 to commemorate the dedication in the same year of the Mount Palomar Observatory.**

Historic games. Every four years the Olympic Games find a home for the season and astound the world with the great achievements of the competitors. And every four years countries everywhere employ postage stamps to commemorate the event and honor the competitors and winners. The stamps are issued well in advance, often carrying a surcharge to help pay for the expense of staging the Games.

At the nineteenth Olympics in Mexico, in 1968, Deborah Meyer of the United States won the two-hundred-meter freestyle and the Republic of Chad paid tribute to her with a stamp that reflects all the energy of her feat *(above, right)*. For the same Games Czechoslovakia *(facing page)* issued a set whose design acknowledges the cultural wealth of the host country, Mexico.

Many years before, for the eighth Olympics held in Paris, in 1924, France issued a stamp *(below, right)* in which the original home of the Games—classical Greece—is remembered.

HRY XIX· OLYMPIÁDY 1968 MEXIKO

40 h

ČESKOSLOVENSKO

J. LIESLER   1968   B. HOUSA

HRY XIX· OLYMPIÁDY 1968 MEXIKO

1,60 KČS

ČESKOSLOVENSKO

J. LIESLER   1968   J. MRÁČEK

HRY XIX· OLYMPIÁDY 1968 MEXIKO

60 h

ČESKOSLOVENSKO

J. LIESLER   1968   J. HERČÍK

HRY XIX· OLYMPIÁDY 1968 MEXIKO

30 h

ČESKOSLOVENSKO

J. LIESLER   1968   B. HOUSA

SEMANA·DE·ARTE·
MODERNA~1922
BRASIL CORREIO 1,00

15c   RF

exposition
internationale
des arts
décoratifs
et industriels
modernes
PARIS
POSTES 1925 FRANCE

EXPOSITION INTERNATIONALE

POSTES   FRANCE

25

DES ARTS
ARIS·1925

DECORATIFS
MODERNES

Arts and crafts. In 1925, the International Exposition of Modern Decorative Arts was held in Paris. It was one of the more important art events of this century, as it gathered together examples of the famous Art Deco style from all over the world. The stamps issued by France for the occasion *(facing page, above, right and below)* are in themselves wonderful exponents of Art Deco design. In 1972 Brazil held her own national festival of modern arts, commemorated by a striking stamp *(facing page, left)*. Also in 1972, Brazil celebrated her 150th anniversary of independence with a set of stamps showing modern national culture *(left)*, including soccer and popular music. Belgium *(below)* issued this stamp in 1970 to mark the twenty-fifth anniversary of her social security system.

Heroes of the time. Two African countries, formerly under French rule, honored the French scientist Louis Pasteur in 1972, 150 years after his birth. Both Gabon *(above, left)* and the Comoro Islands *(left)* showed him surrounded by the trappings of his profession.

Nicaragua *(above)* issued this stamp in 1947 to commemorate her national poet, Ruben Dario. The stamp shows a grieving lion guarding the poet's tomb in Léon Cathedral.

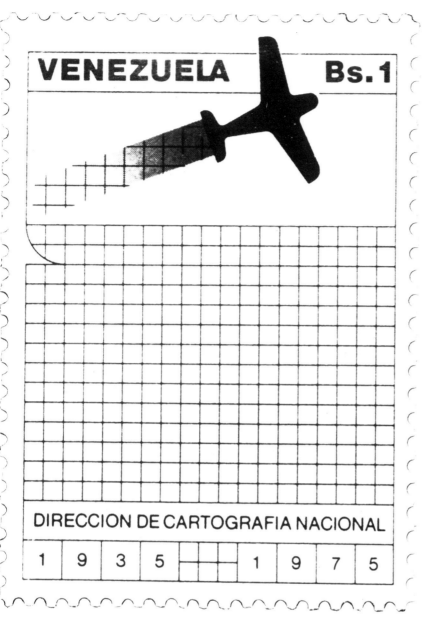

VENEZUELA Bs.1

DIRECCION DE CARTOGRAFIA NACIONAL

| 1 | 9 | 3 | 5 | | | 1 | 9 | 7 | 5 |

The Venezuelan stamp *(above)* uses an aerial map survey for powerful graphic effect to mark the fortieth anniversary of the establishment of the National Cartographic Institute. For the fiftieth anniversary of the first non-stop Atlantic flight by Alcock and Brown, Britain issued this stamp in 1969 *(below)*. The headline report is taken from the newspaper, the *Daily Mail*, which awarded "the men in the machine" what was then a vast 10,000 pounds in prize money. *(By courtesy of the British Post Office)*

FIRST NON-STOP ATLANTIC FLIGHT
ALCOCK & BROWN   14/15 JUNE 1919   5D

STAMP AS STORY-TELLER

Myths, legends, folk tales, and fairy stories have traditionally been handed down from generation to generation by story-tellers and in ballads, poems, and pictures. Recently, these important aspects of a cultural heritage have also been recorded on postage stamps. The stamp as story-teller carries one nation's folk culture all over the world, so that not only are we reminded of our own legendary past but we also come into contact with deities, demigods, and a host of magical beings from distant mythologies. The creation of the world, natural phenomena, and deeply rooted beliefs are explained in countless ways by stories from different parts of the world. There is also a surprising similarity between the various national folk tales; stamps show how many countries have their own Tom Thumb and their own Cinderella, and how many share the fables that saw us through childhood.

"The Legend of Sleepy Hollow" was portrayed on a 1974 stamp *(right)* issued by the United States as a part of an American folklore series. The stamp shows the legendary headless horseman in pursuit of the skeptical Ichabod Crane, under the full moon of a Halloween night.

(Facing page) Story-telling has always been a popular pastime in Africa, and the stories told are of the village and its natural surroundings. This gentle set of stamps from Guinea relates local folk legends about animals with special names, special powers, and special friendships.

LES NIANABLA ET LES CROCODILES

REPUBLIQUE DE GUINEE 40F

«LAN» L'ENFANT-BUFFLE

REPUBLIQUE DE GUINEE 30F

POSTE AERIENNE

«MALISSADIO» LA JEUNE FILLE ET L'HIPPOPOTAME

REPUBLIQUE DE GUINEE 70F

PETITS GENIES DU MONT NIMBA

REPUBLIQUE DE GUINEE 15F

LEUK LE LIEVRE ET LE TAMBOUR

REPUBLIQUE DE GUINEE 50F

Once considered fabulous fiction of the future, many of Jules Verne's predictions have come true in our time. A set of stamps from Monaco translates his stories into modern romantic images, from "Around the World in Eighty Days" *(above)*, to "Twenty Thousand Leagues under the Sea," the tale of the imaginary submarine *Nautilus* after which the U.S.S. *Nautilus* was named *(center and below)*.

(Facing page) In 1971, for the 350th anniversary of the birth of Jean de la Fontaine, several countries issued stamps depicting his much-loved fables. That countries with such varying cultures as Monaco, Niger, and Dahomey should all choose to represent the fables in much the same way shows how universal were the values expressed by la Fontaine in his semi-philosophical but always humorous animal tales.

26

REPUBLIQUE DU NIGER · JEAN DE LA FONTAINE
AERIENNE · 'LE SINGE ET LE LEOPARD'
POSTE 75F

Le singe avait raison ; ce n'est pas sur l'habit
Que la diversité me plaît, c'est dans l'esprit .

DURRENS

1621 MONACO 1971

0.50 · LA FONTAINE

REPUBLIQUE DU NIGER · JEAN DE LA FONTAINE
AERIENNE · "LE LION ET LE RAT"
POSTE 50F

Patience et longueur de temps
Font plus que force ni que rage.

DURRENS

JEAN DE LA FONTAINE 1621-1695
REPUBLIQUE DU DAHOMEY · POSTES · 35F

LE RENARD ET LA CIGOGNE

HALEY

A traditional Japanese folk tale about a Tom Thumb-like character is told in two stamps *(right and facing page, below)*. In one, he uses a wooden bowl as a boat; in the other his ingenuity enables him to conquer the giant.

Two stamps from Mali represent Scheherazade of the *Arabian Nights* telling her stories to the Sultan *(above)* and one of those tales, "Ali Baba and the Forty Thieves" *(facing page, above)*—both designed by a Frenchman, for an African country, in the style of Persian miniatures.

REPUBLIQUE DU MALI

180 F

ALI BABA ET LES QUARANTE VOLEURS

P. LAMBERT

DELRIEU

日本郵便

一寸法師

20 NIPPON

From Laos the beautiful
Goddess Nangkinnali *(facing
page)* and from Greece *(below)* a
set of scenes from classical
mythology. The images for these
stamps were taken from unique
sources—including an ancient
Greek vase, a classical amphora,
and the Pergamun altar.

This set of stamps from Thailand *(right)* was issued for International Letter Writing Week of 1976. It shows Garuda, the messenger of the gods, and two other figures from Eastern religious mythology.

Animal lore. Tibet used the symbol of the Snow Lion on all her stamps, such as this 1933 issue *(left)*. It was an obvious choice since according to legend the Buddha was accompanied on his travels by a small dog who, in dangerous situations, would protect his master by turning himself into a fierce lion. The Japanese stamp *(below)* is based on a comic scroll by an eleventh-century artist. The story represented by the laughing frogs is now obscure, but the stamp, issued in 1977, tells us that comics were already popular in medieval Japan.

AIRMAIL—CONQUEST OF THE SKIES

It was not until after the First World War that postal services began to experiment with the transportation of everyday mail by air. Flying machines were still simple and slow—primitive compared to today's supersonic jets—but they were nevertheless capable of carrying mail at speeds far greater than those achieved by boat or train. By the beginning of the 1920s the airplane had been tested in battle, and a world vastly changed by war demanded this speed of communication.

The earliest airmail stamps were regular designs roughly overprinted—often with a simple airplane motif—and usually marked "experimental," since the first mail flights were essentially trial runs from one city to another within one country. The first stamp designed specifically for airmail use was the United States' "Jenny" of 1918. It was issued for an experimental airmail service between Washington D.C. and New York, with one stop at Philadelphia.

Early airmails generally showed some form of contemporary airplane. Though they now look like antiques, these planes were at the time the latest in modernity, and airmail stamp designers delighted in bird's-eye views where the amazing flying machine was set against a vast, swimming scene of old buildings and ancient landscapes. Of course, each major event in the history of flight has been celebrated on airmails—including Lindbergh's pioneering effort and other outstanding flights. The German Zeppelins were celebrated wherever they went, and more recently space flight has figured prominently on airmail stamps.

The "Jenny" *(below)* **issued by the United States in 1918, was the first specially designed airmail stamp. It shows an early and famous flying machine, the Curtiss Jenny. The stamp has achieved a certain fame, and particularly the block shown here in which the centers of the stamps were mistakenly inverted during printing. The block was bought in 1918 as part of a whole sheet of a hundred "inverts," by a Mr. W. Robey. The unique stamps quickly gained in value. Robey sold his sheet for $15,000 and a block such as the one shown is now valued at $400,000. A single stamp from the renowned sheet recently sold at auction for $130,000.** *(Photo courtesy Raymond H. Weill, New Orleans)*

(Facing page) **Early airmails of the 1920s and 30s from several countries, each showing a plane and the local landscape —including the Great Wall of China and the Egyptian Pyramids. Many of these stamps are "first" airmails from their respective countries.** *(Reference collection, Philatelic Foundation, New York)*

Allegories of flight. In the early days of airmail, many stamps captured the exuberance of flight with far-fetched but often magnificent allegorical designs. Winging birds were an obvious choice of image. Other stamps drew comparisons with mythical characters, such as Icarus, whose wax wings touched the sun and melted; Pegasus, the winged horse; and the fabulous Centaur. *(Reference collection, Philatelic Foundation, New York)*

The symbolic treatment of airmail stamp design continues in modern times. The Ryukyu Islands *(right)* depicts a flying goddess while Dahomey *(below, right and left)* has chosen the Venus de Milo to honor the Mariner 5 and Venus 4 space probes of 1968. The stamps were overprinted in 1969 to celebrate the Moon landing in July of that year.

Valuable firsts. The delicate Greek stamps *(left)* are the first airmails from that country. Issued in 1926, they show classical Greek scenes and the inevitable, toy-like airplane. *(Collection, Richard Beresford)*

In 1920 the private *Compañia Colombiana de Navegacion* ran Colombia's first airmail service under contract to the government. The stamps issued for this service *(below)* have a child-like appeal. But the simple, naive designs are deceptive—the four stamps are now worth about $10,000. *(Collection, Alex Rendon)*

This stylized, typically Art Deco design *(right)* was issued as an airmail in 1931 by Curaçao in the Netherlands Antilles. The stamp shows Mercury, speedy messenger of the gods.

Switzerland issued this bold airmail stamp *(below)* in 1923. *(Reference collection, Philatelic Foundation, New York)*

The history of flight. Early airmail stamps were conceived with a lively sense of flight's long and varied history. Italy, in a 1932 stamp *(above)*, did not forget her own Leonardo da Vinci who, in the distant fourteenth century, invented an incredibly advanced flying machine. Cyrenaica *(center)*, in 1934, honors the flight to Italy of the Graf Zeppelin and Russia *(below)* publicizes two events with one robust stamp—the 1930 flight of the Graf Zeppelin from Germany to Moscow, and the completion of a Soviet five-year industrial plan in four years. *(Reference collection, Philatelic Foundation, New York)*

The development of airplane design is reflected in successive airmail stamps. This from the Island of Réunion, off Africa (*right*) shows a powerful 50s jet descending through clouds. In 1969 France *(below)* celebrated the first flight of her much prized, supersonic Concorde.

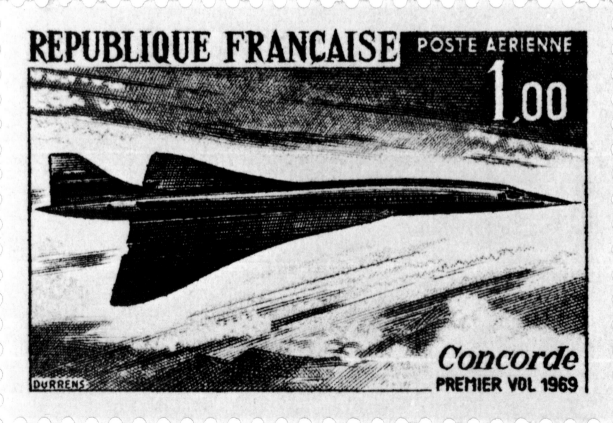

Stars and Stripes. America honors Amelia Earhart *(above)*, the first woman to fly the Atlantic. The stamp was issued in 1963—twenty-six years after Earhart disappeared on a Pacific flight.

Two striking airmail stamp designs *(left)* from the United States—a 1976 stamp with globes cleverly disguised as engines *(Collection, Peter Robertson)*; and in 1968 a fifty-star runway representing the fifty states of the U.S.A. *(Collection, Richard Beresford)*

CRUSADERS

It should be possible to follow the political and social history of any country through its postage stamps. From empire to kingdom, through revolution to independence or republic, jubilant nations always commemorate their struggles and victories on stamps. With liberation and its anniversaries comes an outburst of dramatic stamps bearing that familiar symbol of freedom, the broken chain. And while the struggles continue all over the world, other nations, secure in their freedom, emphasize their progress against discrimination by issuing stamps dedicated to the causes of minority groups and to the rights of the people as a whole.

Several nations issue semi-postal or charity stamps, where a surcharge added to the regular rate of postage is given to recognized charity organizations. The first semi-postal stamps were issued by Russia, in 1905, after the Russo-Japanese war, in aid of her wounded and her orphans. In the following year Holland and Romania followed suit. Soon Belgium, France, Monaco, Germany, and Switzerland were issuing semi-postal stamps for such diverse causes as the Red Cross, the fight against tuberculosis, youth programs, old-age support, war veterans, and hospitals. Millions in funds have been raised in this way, particularly after the two world wars.

To breathe free . . . The Statue of Liberty is a powerful symbol of the crusading spirit. It has special significance for Americans and for the people of France who contributed $250,000 in order to give the statue to the United States as a centennial commemoration of the nations' alliance during the American Revolution. The stamp *(facing page)* was issued by France, in 1936, as a semi-postal, the surcharge going to the aid of political refugees—in perfect harmony with the meaning of the statue on whose pedestal are inscribed the words: "Give me your tired, your poor,/Your huddled masses yearning to breathe free. . . ."

The United States stamps of 1975 *(below)* show the dome of the Capitol Building in Washington D.C. and the Liberty Bell housed in Independence Hall, Philadelphia.

Fighting for freedom. When, in 1952, Egypt became a republic instead of a kingdom under the leadership of King Farouk, she issued these celebratory stamps full of symbols of a free Egypt *(above and right)*.

(Facing page) The Polish stamp *(above)* was issued in 1960 to commemorate the 550th anniversary of the great Battle of Grunwald, in which the Polish King Wladyslaw Jagiello and his troops fought against the Teutonic knights. The stamp, showing a painting of the battle scene by J. Matejko, is probably unique in that 800 people are depicted in miniature format.

To mark the thirtieth anniversary of the intervention of the International Brigades in Spain, Czechoslovakia issued this stamp (*bottom*) showing Pablo Picasso's famous painting, *Guernica*. Picasso painted *Guernica* as a giant mural depicting the horror of the destruction of that Spanish town bombed by German planes in 1937 during the Spanish Civil War. *(Collection, Richard Beresford)*

WOMAN SUFFRAGE

1920·1970

RIGHT TO VOTE

VOTES FOR WOMEN

50TH ANNIVERSARY

U.S. 6¢

FREEDOM OF THE PRESS

U.S. POSTAGE 4¢

COMBAT RACISM

United Nations 25¢

0,20 +0,10 REPUBLIQUE FRANÇAISE POSTES +

G. ROUAULT   J. PIEL

FÜR KAMPFAKTIONEN GEGEN RASSISMUS

JOHN HEARTFIELD 1937

UND RASSENDISKRIMINIERUNG

35 DDR

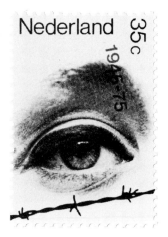

Man's inhumanity to man. These semi-postal stamps, (*above and left*) issued by France, Belgium, and Holland in 1964, 1965, and 1975, tell the dramatic story of the end of World War II when the chains and fences holding prisoners of war were broken, deportees returned home, and the concentration camps were liberated.

(*Facing page*) Stamps committed to the righting of wrongs or dedicated to a good cause tend to carry their message prominently in a bold design—as shown in this selection from several countries. The East German stamp (*below, left*), issued in support of the 1971 Year Against Racial Discrimination, is given added meaning by the use of raised fists portrayed by John Heartfield, the radical artist renowned for his powerful political posters of the 1920s. It contrasts strongly with the softness of the French stamp (*below, right*), issued in 1961 as a semi-postal in aid of the Red Cross—to which many stamps have been dedicated. France has often chosen works by famous artists to enhance the appeal of her charity stamps. This one shows a painting by Georges Rouault, *It Would Be So Lovely to Love.*

Cambodia, known as The Republic of Khmer, issued this stamp *(above)* in 1971 to publicize territorial defense. The two Algerian stamps *(center)*, showing soldiers in battle and a local woman comforting the wounded, were issued in 1966 to commemorate the Moslem Volunteers, or *Moudjahid,* who fought a guerrilla war against France for independence.

In 1950, the World Federation of Trade Unions met in Budapest, and the Hungarian government issued this stamp *(below)* to publicize the convention.

Glory, Peace, Victory, and Tranquillity are rendered symbolically on this set of stamps from Brazil *(facing page)*, issued in 1945 to celebrate the victory of the allied nations in Europe.

TWENTIETH CENTURY— THE ROAD TO SPACE

At the turn of the century, progress became a by-word of the Western World—progress in science and technology, in agriculture, in communications, and in the social spheres of education, housing, and leisure. Each new discovery, invention, or triumph of man over nature has been celebrated on the postage stamp. The twentieth century has culminated in space exploration and research. All over the world nations have shared in space-mania by issuing stamps to commemorate successive triumphs.

The stamps in this section reflect our century's monumental preoccupation with progress. They show how the world has been drawn together by shared ambitions and by sophisticated methods of communication. All the excitement of the modern age is captured in these dynamic designs. They are the index of national and global optimism.

Stratosphere to space. Progress is by definition a moving force, and by nature relative. The Belgian stamp *(facing page)* marks the early days in a century of progress. Issued in 1932, it celebrates scientific advance by honoring Professor Auguste Piccard, whose balloon made two ascents into the stratosphere, in 1931 and 1932, with many scientific instruments on board. *(Courtesy Frank Warner, New York)*

By 1975 progress lay in space and in international cooperation. The four stamps *(below)* were issued simultaneously by Russia and the United States to celebrate their first combined space effort—the Apollo-Soyuz link-up.

TV age. Communications media have become the mainstay of modern life, both for governments and for individuals. In the mid-1950s television became the world's new wonder. Italy *(below, right)* issued this bold stamp in 1954 to commemorate the inception of Italian television. A map of Italy is shown on the screen. The following year, France issued her own television stamp *(right)* to publicize advances in the medium. TV waves radiate from the Eiffel Tower and are received by antennae sprouting from surrounding rooftops.

In August 1960 the nations of the world were linked by the first communications satellite, Echo 1, which was placed into orbit by NASA. The event was commemorated by the American stamp *(below)* with an optimistic bid for peace among the nations to be linked. The dramatic Russian stamp *(facing page)* was issued in 1974 to celebrate space stations Mars 4 to 7—a series of communications satellites operating on a relay system.

ИЗУЧЕНИЕ ПЛАНЕТ
СОЛНЕЧНОЙ СИСТЕМЫ ПРОДОЛЖАЕТСЯ
МАРС-4
МАРС-5
МАРС-6
МАРС-7
1974
6к
ПОЧТА СССР

Into space. The United States and Russia, leaders in the space race, have issued numerous stamps to commemorate victories in exploration and discovery. Other nations have contributed memorable designs reflecting the sheer excitement of space travel. The United States stamp (*above, left*) commemorates the success of the Apollo 8 mission of 1968, which put the first men into orbit around the Moon. The stamp shows the distant planet Earth appearing over the Moon's horizon. The words "In the beginning . . ." are a reminder of the moving words from Genesis that were read to the world on Christmas Eve by the orbiting astronauts of Apollo 8.

Mexico (*above, right*) honors the first landing of American astronauts on the Moon, in July 1969. The photograph of the footprint has become a powerfully symbolic image of man's first step on the lunar landscape. The first dog in space is depicted by Romania, in 1963 (*below*). The dog, Laika, was sent up in the Russian spacecraft Sputnik 2 as part of an early research mission.

Three American stamps (*facing page, above and below, right*) document the national space adventure: Project Mercury, the first orbital flight by an American astronaut, in 1962; Gemini 4 and the first American space walk, in 1967; and the Skylab space research project of 1974, looking forward to the space shuttle and possibilities of space colonies. Also in 1974, Russia depicts the rocket blastoff that carried spacecraft Soyuz into space to link up with the American Apollo team (*below, left*).

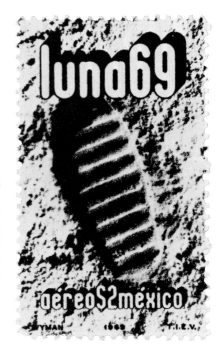

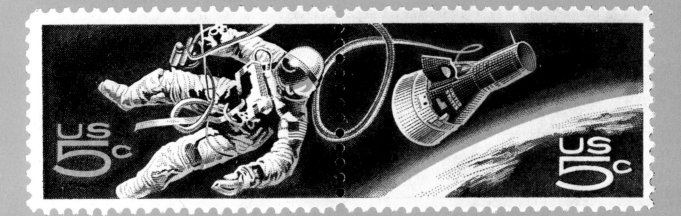

The United States in 1933 commemorates the famous Graf Zeppelin trans-Atlantic flight of the same year. The 50-cent stamp *(above)*, issued as part of a Century of Progress series to mark the 1938-1939 New York World's Fair with that theme, was considered expensive at the time. As the years progressed, the stamp's value increased and in 1979 it is priced at $110. *(Reference collection, Philatelic Foundation, New York)*

In 1951 Bulgaria celebrates her first tractor *(center)*, in the service of communal agriculture and its advancement.

France *(below)* shows a "modern" electric locomotive to mark the thirteenth International Railway Congress of 1937 which was held in Paris.

(Facing page) China, in this 1955 stamp *(below, left)*, draws attention to national developments in electric power with a high-tension pylon, once a symbol of modernity. And in 1970, Cyprus *(below, right)* marks International Education Year with an emblem generated by computer. The "computer head" appeared on stamps from several countries in the same year, stressing the link between good education and technological advance. In 1961, influenced by progress in the West and in Russia, Egypt implemented a ten-year plan moving towards modern industrialization. This stamp *(above)* marks the inception of that plan with effusive optimism.

Where science ends. Stamps of the modern age have increasingly acknowledged the influence of man and of nature on the abstract workings of science. Here, for instance, we have a 1957 stamp issued by the United States *(above)* in commemoration of International Geophysical Year. The design, used also by the United Nations and several other countries, shows the solar disc and behind it hands from Michelangelo's *Creation of Adam*—a fascinating fusion of religious and scientific emblems.

From Czechoslovakia *(center)*, a stamp of 1965, publicizing space research and the Year of the Quiet Sun—a year without sunspots and therefore with minimal atmospheric disturbances on communications.

The stamp from Pakistan *(below)* is designed to call attention to the nation's first nuclear power plant. And Mexico *(facing page)*, in a startling adaptation of da Vinci's man, celebrates the tenth anniversary of the Agreement of Tlatelolco which banned nuclear arms in Latin America. *(Facing page, collection, Richard Beresford)*

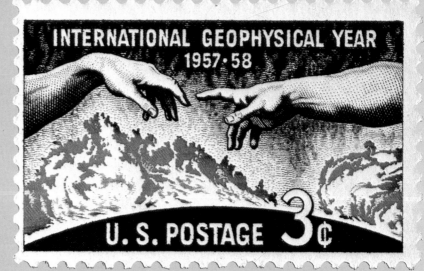

TRATADO DE
TLATELOLCO
1967 1977

MEXICO $1.60 AEREO

H. RODRIGUEZ   T. I. E. V.   1977

EGYPTE مصر
1947-١٩٤٧
المعرض الدولي
للفنون الجميلة الحديثة
EXPOSITION INTERNATIO: NALE D'ART CONTEMPORAIN
30 +30 MILLS
POSTES بريد
٣٠+٣٠ مليما

ROOTS—A GLIMPSE OF THE PAST

The historic founding of a great city, traces of prehistory, memories of the still recent past—distances in time both near and far are traveled by the world of stamps. In modern times the need to establish roots and preserve traditions has become increasingly important. Individual nations stress their individuality and evoke a national pride by recording their past on stamps. The sophistication of early civilizations is often emphasized by countries such as Greece, Egypt, and China, while others look back to the relative peace and simplicity of an earlier life. Of course, few people can resist the occasional bout of nostalgia. Many stamps take a sentimental journey into the recent past, touching our living memory with old cars we might have owned, old trains we might have ridden in, and other objects that shock us out of our time and into another.

The famous bust of Nefertiti (facing page), powerful queen and wife of the Pharaoh Ikhnaton, is a noble representation of Egypt's great past. The bust—made in the queen's lifetime—has been acclaimed as one of the greatest art masterpieces of all time. No wonder, then, that it was chosen by Egypt for a stamp in 1947, when she hosted the International Exhibition of Contemporary Art.

In 1953 New York City celebrated her 300th birthday. The anniversary was marked by this evocative stamp (left) showing a Dutch ship in the harbor of what was then known as New Amsterdam, with a shadow of the future in the background.

Discovering lost worlds.
Prehistory holds an uncanny
fascination. As its mysteries are
fathomed by scientists and
historians, we are able to shape
an idea of our distant ancestry,
which has left us a legacy of
pictures. Rock paintings not only
give us a remarkable insight into
prehistoric life, but are early and
beautiful examples of man's
creative impulse. Among the
many stamps issued on the
theme of rock paintings, the
stamps from Lesotho *(above)*
depict prehistoric animals,
early man, and the relationship
between the two. The designs of
the stamps are taken from actual
rock paintings found in various
regions of Lesotho and show
how elegantly stone-age
bushmen represented their own
lives. Many prehistoric elements
have been found near Lake
Nyassa in Malawi, including
these lyrical rock paintings
(below, right) issued as a set in
1972.

Ages of animal *(facing page)*.
The United States set *(above)*
was issued in 1970 as part of a
natural history series, in
connection with the 1969 to 1970
commemoration of the centenary
of the American Museum of
Natural History in New York City.
The Congo stamps *(below)* were
issued in 1975, in recognition of
the popular appeal of prehistoric
animals.

LESOTHO 10c

archers

LESOTHO

running hunters 3c

LESOTHO

hunting scene 25c

MALAWI

Figures (Chencherere Hill)

ROCK PAINTINGS 3t

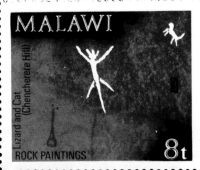

MALAWI

Lizard and Cat (Chencherere Hill)

ROCK PAINTINGS 8t

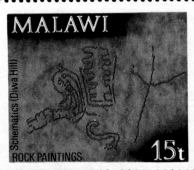

MALAWI

Schematics (Diwa Hill)

ROCK PAINTINGS 15t

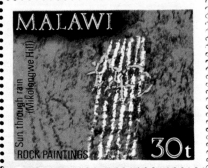

MALAWI

Sun through rain (Mikolongwe Hill)

ROCK PAINTINGS 30t

U.S. 6c

AMERICAN BALD EAGLE

U.S. 6c

AFRICAN ELEPHANT HERD

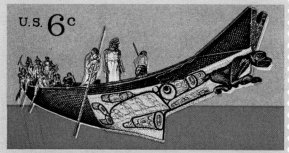

U.S. 6c

HAIDA CEREMONIAL CANOE

U.S. 6c

THE AGE OF REPTILES

REPUBLIQUE POPULAIRE
DU CONGO

POSTES 1975

95 F

CRYPTOCLEIDUS

RÉPUBLIQUE DU CONGO

TYRANNOSAURUS

75 F

POPULAIRE

POSTES 1975

RÉPUBLIQUE DU CONGO

MOSCHOPS

55 F

POPULAIRE

POSTES 1975

Primitive peace. For many nations, and particularly those still developing towards industrialization, the simplicity of pastoral life is only now becoming history. Morocco *(above)* issued this stamp in 1939, showing a native goatherd, and the stamp from French Guiana *(below)*, showing a Carib archer as a symbol of that land's inhabitants and their lives, was issued in 1929.

Glorious Motherland. The stamps from China *(facing page)* were issued during 1952 and 1953 as part of a series designed to stimulate national pride by glorifying China's past. Entitled "Glorious Motherland," the set features inventions by ancient and medieval Chinese scientists—including the oldest compass, from the third century B.C.; an astronomical instrument from the Ming Dynasty; and a drum cart to measure distances, from the Ching Dynasty.

Nostalgia trips. The progress of locomotion from 1812 to 1865 is shown in this set of stamps *(this page)* issued in 1964 by the tiny European country of San Marino. The antique engines, with their optimistic names like "Rocket" and "Spitfire" and their tidy puffs of smoke, are a simple evocation of a bygone age.

Monaco is home of one of the greatest auto events in the world, the Monte Carlo Rally, and for this reason has issued many sets of car stamps. This set *(facing page)*, issued in 1975, describes the evolution of the motor car from 1900 to 1975 with a characteristic impression of speed.

MONACO 0,50 1975

VOISIN V12 - 1930

MONACO 0,20 1975

isotta fraschini 8A.1928

J.COMBET

MONACO 0,30 1975

CORD L.29

DURRENS

MONACO 0,60 1975

DUESENBERG «SJ» 1933

BETEMPS

MONACO 0,85 1975

DELAHAYE 135 M.1940

GUILLAME

MONACO 1,20 1975

CISITALIA - Pininfarina 1946

BETEMPS

1975 0,05 MONACO

ROLLS-ROYCE 1907 "SILVER GHOST"

FORGET

MONACO 5,50 1975

LAMBORGHINI - Bertone "COUNTACH" 1974

FORGET

CHANGING FACES

What links the histories of John F. Kennedy, Lenin, Queen Victoria, Winston Churchill, and Emperor Bokassa? As heads of state and public figures, they and several other monarchs, presidents, and national figures have been portrayed again and again on postage stamps. Their faces have appeared so often in this miniature format that the progression of their lives, their fate and fame, can be traced—even from childhood.

This fascinating aspect of the stamp world takes various forms. During a long reign, a King or Queen may be portrayed at regular intervals, so that one monarch's changing face is recorded forever on a series of stamps. In some cases a whole set of stamps is issued at one time, giving a narrative record of an important leader's life and career.

Vladimir Ilyich Lenin, founding father of the Soviet Republic, died in 1924. Ten years later Russia issued a set of stamps to mourn their "Ten Years Without Lenin." This nostalgic set shows him as a child, a student, an adult, and an orator. The same stamps were brought out again in 1944 as "Twenty Years Without Lenin" *(left)*.

(*Facing page*) King Alphonso XIII of Spain was born king in 1886, six months after his father's untimely death. His mother remained regent until he reached the age of sixteen, but as king it was his portrait that was used on contemporary stamps. And so we have the monarch as a baby in 1889, as a cadet in 1901, as a young king, aged twenty-three in 1909, and as a mature man of thirty-six in 1922. These stamps, issued over a period of thirty-six years, show how a succession of individual issues can combine to tell a remarkable story.
(*Reference collection, Philatelic Foundation, New York*)

Biography in miniature.
Queen Victoria, whose portrait as a young girl appears on the world's first postage stamp, came to the throne in 1837 at the age of sixteen. She reigned for sixty-four years until her death in 1901. Not only Britain, but all the countries of her vast empire used her portrait on stamps, particularly at significant points during her life as queen. The most famous portrayal of Victoria is the elegant Chalon portrait painted not long after she ascended the throne. It was used on British colony stamps during her long reign, and even distant countries of the Commonwealth such as Van Diemen's Land—now part of Australia—created primitive interpretations of the queen's portrait as in the 1853 stamp *(below, left)*. In 1897 New South Wales issued a stamp *(right)* showing a simplified portrait of the queen as a widow. And in the same year, for a Jubilee issue to mark the sixtieth year of Victoria's reign, Canada issued a stamp *(below, right)* showing both the early Chalon portrait and a later face probably adapted from a photograph of 1897, with the queen as empress wearing the imperial crown. *(Reference collection, Philatelic Foundation, New York)*

Winston Churchill's adventurous life has been recorded on stamps from several countries *(facing page)*. Because his death in 1965 occurred only nine years before the 100th anniversary of his birth, one decade saw the issuance of a vast range of commemorative stamps that trace his career through war and peace. A stamp issued in 1974 by Aitutaki *(above, left)* shows him age five in Dublin; also in 1974 Antigua issued a stamp *(below)* commemorating one of his adventures as a reporter during the Boer War, when he was taken prisoner but managed to escape. The stamp shows the warrant for his arrest and a map of his escape route. The United States, which made Churchill the only honorary American citizen by Act of Congress, chose a well-known portrait of Churchill by the famous photographer of the famous, Karsh, for a stamp issued to honor the British statesman shortly after his death *(above, right)*.

CENTENARY OF THE BIRTH OF SIR WINSTON CHURCHILL 30 November 1974

10c AITUTAKI
COOK ISLANDS

CHURCHILL

U.S. **5** CENTS

SIR WINSTON CHURCHILL
EꟾꟾR

$1

CENTENARY OF THE BIRTH OF

Pietersburg
TRANSVAAL
Pretoria   Lourenco
                  Marques
ESCAPE
ROUTE

AMBUSH   NATAL

Durban

£25
(Twenty-five Pounds stg.) REWARD is offered by the
Sub-Commission of the fifth division, on behalf of the Special Constable
of the said division, to anyone who brings the escaped prisoner of war

CHURCHILL,
dead or alive to this office.

For the Sub-Commission of the fifth division,
(Signed) LODK. de HAAS, Sec.

ANTIGUA

COLONEL JEAN BEDEL BOKASSA
PRESIDENT DE LA REPUBLIQUE
DELRIEU

In 1958 a small French colony in Equatorial Africa proclaimed itself the Central African Republic. The new nation, later found to be rich in oil and uranium, embarked on a quick road to wealth. In 1977 the country proclaimed itself an empire and former President for Life Jean Bedel Bokassa crowned himself Emperor Bokassa I. In his new role, Bokassa surrounded himself with all the lavish ceremonial trappings of a mighty leader, and he became an international personality overnight. Stamps from the Central African Republic (*above and center, right*) show the evolution of a Napoleonic ruler. He is seen as President, simply dressed, planting a cotton bush to publicize his development plan, "Operation Bokassa"; he is seen as Colonel Bokassa, two years after taking over as head of state in 1966; and he is seen finally crowned in splendor, as Emperor Bokassa I.

(*Facing page and below, right*) John F. Kennedy was a leader who won the affection of the

world. No wonder, then, that countries everywhere have issued stamps to honor him. The Malagasy stamp (*this page, below, right*) was issued in 1973 for the tenth anniversary of his death. The more informal set (*facing page*) was issued by the Middle Eastern Sheikdom of Fujeira only two years after the president's death, and it was obviously designed to touch a thousand hearts. The set tells the Kennedy story, showing him as a boy, as a naval lieutenant, as an orator, and in a familiar portrait from his brief term as president. Other stamps in the set show him at other stages in his public and private life, as statesman and as family man. The neat black cancellations on these stamps, combined with the fact that they are still fully gummed, implies that they have never been used in the mail, and confirms that this set was intended less for postal use than to collect revenue through vast sales to collectors and Kennedy lovers. Incidentally, such "cancelled to order" stamps are considered quite worthless by serious stamp collectors.

ART STAMPS

It is sometimes claimed that many postage stamps are miniature works of art, designed, engraved, and printed as they are by major craftsmen known widely in the world of stamp collecting. And so, when a stamp carries on its face an image of an art work, we encounter a doubly demanding situation; the design or "art" of the stamp becomes more than ever a careful and crucial factor. A boom in art stamps occurred in the 1930s. Countries renowned for their art treasures had reproduced art on charity stamps before this, but suddenly nearly every country in the world began to reproduce masterpieces by Michelangelo and da Vinci by the score, often with strange results.

The stamps that follow focus on individual nations' celebrations of their own artistic wealth, from the ancient cave paintings of Chad to modern French masterpieces and American folk art.

Korea *(facing page)* adopts a well-known eighteenth-century Korean painting, *Man Contemplating Book,* for a truly modern yet harmonious stamp design.

In 1967 the Bailloud Expedition discovered these cave paintings *(left)* in the Ennedi mountain range of Chad.

(Pages 78 and 79) Bhutan's ancient and sacred art form is the Tankha—a painted wall hanging kept in temples or monasteries depicting scenes from the life of Buddha. The stamps on page 78 show the Tankha form used for modern stamps printed on silk. *(Collection, Richard Beresford)*

France, one of the art centers of the world, issued a series of art stamps spanning several years and featuring works by major French painters. Here *(page 79)* we see the lyrical *Married Couple with Eiffel Tower* by Marc Chagall, one of France's most loved modern artists.

REPUBLIQUE FRANÇAISE

0.85

1963

M.CHAGALL

POSTES

American art. The United States has issued several stamps that show the diversity of American arts, stretching back to the folk art of Hopi pottery *(right)*. Another stamp *(facing page, below)* commemorates the 1968 opening of the National Portrait Gallery, Washington, D.C., and honors the American Indian. It shows a portrait by Cyrenius Hall of Chief Joseph, or Thunder Traveling over Mountains, the intrepid and steadfast chief of the Nez Percé who in 1877 led his tribe through a 1700-mile running battle against the U.S. Army.

National Dance Week, April 1978, was marked by the United States stamps *(facing page, above)* showing various forms that have made American dance famous. This block was among the few that escaped inspection by the post office. The obvious misperforations make it both intriguing and highly prized as a rarity now worth $100 instead of the original 52 cents. *(Collection, Viola Ilma, copyright USPS)*

The Aztec calendar *(below)* or "Piedra del Sol" was chosen for this Mexican stamp of 1973 as part of a long series on Mexican art and science. *(Collection, Richard Beresford)*

Hopi: Heard Museum Phoenix

Pueblo Art USA 13c

Acoma: School of American Research

Pueblo Art USA 13c

Zia: Museum of New Mexico

Pueblo Art USA 13c

San Ildefonso: Denver Art Museum

Pueblo Art USA 13c

For Easter, 1974, Guiana issued this strikingly simple stamp *(right)* presenting the Crucifixion in pre-Columbian style.

The delicate brushstrokes of *Galloping Horses (facing page)* were painted by the twentieth-century artist Chu Pei Hong. The stamps were issued as a set by the People's Republic of China in 1978. *(Collection, Viola Ilma)*

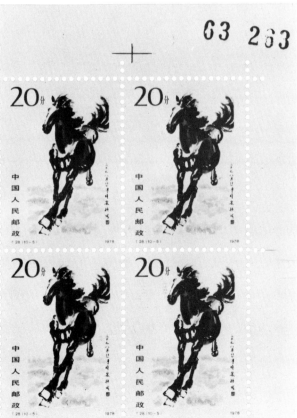

Another from France's series of art stamps, this one *(facing page)* features *Circus* by the nineteenth-century Neo-Impressionist Georges Seurat. *(Collection, Richard Beresford)*

The Tunisian stamps *(above and right)* show ancient Roman mosaics.

BACK TO NATURE

There is nothing so important to urban man, and yet so neglected by him, as his natural environment, which provides him with food, fuel, and escape from city pressures. Stamps are a constant reminder of nature's wealth. From all over the world they come emblazoned with butterflies, birds, fish, animals— all those exotic, enviable colors and graceful forms. The landscape, too, has long been a favorite subject for stamps. Desert, forest, jungle, and green field take us on a tour of the continents.

Every country in the world wants to show off its natural beauty in flora and fauna, and the postage stamp is one of the most effective means of doing so. Nature stamps of every description beckon the tourist to far corners of the earth. But few nations can present an entirely ideal view of their environment. Even in the underdeveloped countries of the Third World, nature is endangered by industrialization. In the past ten years, stamps from many nations have spoken out, often forcefully, on several aspects of environmental concern.

New nation, ancient land *(facing page)*. Having gained independence from France in 1961, Algeria issued in the following year its first set of stamps as a new nation. The set of five included this depiction of one of the area's natural highlights—the famous Gorge de Kerrata—and the rugged, mountainous territory surrounding it. A sweep of modern road across the landscape is carefully set against the peace of man and donkey who follow a more ancient path. Ironically this stamp—one of the first to bear the Arabic inscription for the new republic—was part of a French set originally issued in 1960.

All-American trees *(left)*. Growing over 320 feet into the sky, with a lifespan of more than 2000 years, it is no wonder that the United States chose its native sequoia as one subject for a set of tree stamps. The sequoia is the most spectacular of American trees. The fact that it was named in honor of Sequoya, or George Guess, a Cherokee Indian and creator of a tribal written language, gives this tree a particular national significance. The white pine is a dwarf by comparison, but it is one of North America's most important timber trees. *(Copyright USPS)*

87

Preserving the environment.
Four years after independence
Zambia was struck by her
responsibility for the national
environment. These stamps
(facing page) stress three
aspects of conservation
essential to this African
country's well being. Bordered
on all sides by land, Zambia is
dependent on clean rivers. Good
crops can only be ensured by
correct tilling and, as always, the
tree must be protected both for
use and to hold the soil.
(Collection, Viola Ilma)

The Monaco stamp *(right)* is
concerned not so much with
man's use of nature as with
his effect on the voiceless
animal and bird population
alongside which he lives. This
disturbing stamp is designed to
shock people into the fight
against pollution of the oceans
by oil. It shows quite ruthlessly
the fatal effect on any bird of
such pollution.

(Above) Costa Rica, 1937. This stamp, showing Costa Rica's national flower, the orchid, was issued for the National Industrial and Agricultural Exhibition, in San José. (Collection, Richard Beresford)

(Below) Monaco, 1959. One of a series of nine flower stamps. (Collection, Richard Beresford)

Nature, the divine order (facing page). Oriental nature scenes have a particular beauty. And these stylized depictions of birds, flowers, animals, and landscapes are perfectly suited to miniaturization in the postage stamp.

The stamp (above, right) from the People's Republic of China bears the personal seal or "chop" of its designer, the People's artist Wu Tso-Jen. Near his seal, Chinese characters describe the scene in typical poetic matter-of-factness: "Giant panda leaning against bamboo eating leaves." Here, China is rightfully honoring its native and much-loved panda. Zoos in Washington, London, and Moscow received pandas from China, their only natural habitat, and the World Wildlife Fund has adopted the panda, an endangered species, as its symbol.

(Above, left) A truly Japanese design based on a painting bearing all the national characteristics of delicate exoticism. This stamp was well chosen to spread the name of Japan in International Letter Writing Week, 1977.

90

The stamp *(below)* from Taiwan was issued in 1970 to coordinate the Chinese Cultural Campaign and the protection of domestic animals. It may seem strange, then, that the stamp is based on a scroll painting, *One Hundred Horses,* by an eighteenth-century Italian missionary. But Giuseppe Castiglione, later named Lang Shih-ning when he was appointed court painter in China, soon learned to incorporate that Chinese spirit of vitality into his work. The depth of this painting reflects Chinese philosophical ideas of the Great Void.

Tristan da Cunha, 1974 *(right)*. It's possible that on this tiny island in the South Atlantic Ocean, the rockhopper penguin—shown here as master of the beaches—outnumbers the human population of 270 men, women, and children.

(Facing page) Gambia *(left)* publicizes her two most important crops—palm oil and rice—while Jersey *(right)* remembers her nineteenth-century farming with evocative relics—farm implements now safely housed in the local museum of agriculture.

Tristan da Cunha · Rockhopper and egg · E II R · 2½p

Tristan da Cunha · Rockhopper penguins fishing · E II R · 7½p

Tristan da Cunha · Rockhopper penguin and fledgling · E II R · 25p

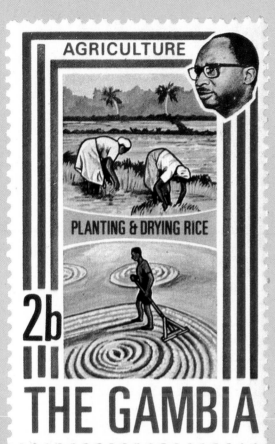

AGRICULTURE

PLANTING & DRYING RICE

2b

THE GAMBIA

2b AGRICULTURE

OIL PALM

The Gambia

JERSEY

CIDER CRUSHER (Tou d'Preinseu)

Nineteenth Century Farming

3½ p

G. DRUMMOND   1975   COURVOISIER S.A.

JERSEY

POTATO DIGGER (Tchéthue à Défoui)

Nineteenth Century Farming

3 p

G. DRUMMOND   1975   COURVOISIER S.A.

JERSEY

6-HORSE PLOUGH (Le Grand 'Tchéthue)

Nineteenth Century Farming

8 p

G. DRUMMOND   1975   COURVOISIER S.A.

Watching woods and trees.
Judging by the stamp *(above)*
issued by Austria in 1967, trees
have long been recognized as
environmentally important.
Austria is honoring with this
stamp the centenary of the
National Academy of the Science
of Forestry and its endeavor to
understand the limits of
growth—the tree-line.
(Collection, Richard Beresford)
In 1960 the fifth World Forestry
Congress was held in Seattle,
Washington. The stamp from
Tunisia *(right)* marks this
occasion.

**Indigenous species, a
nation's pride** *(facing page).*
On December 28, 1959, Niger
issued its first stamp as an
autonomous republic. This
stamp *(right)* shows the
strangely beautiful crested
crane, a native bird, and calls for
its protection. Mauritania *(left)*
takes the proud cheetah, fastest
cat in the world, for one of a set
of twelve stamps showing
indigenous animals. St. Pierre et
Miquelon *(below)*—two small
islands off the Southern coast of
Newfoundland—promote
tourism in 1969 with a depiction
of wild horses on an equally wild
coastline.

94

DE MAURITANIE

RÉPUBLIQUE ISLAMIQUE

1F50

POSTES

GUEPARD

RÉPUBLIQUE DU NIGER

1F

POSTES

GRUES COURONNEES

PROTECTION DE LA FAUNE

RF

POSTE AERIENNE

SAINT-PIERRE ET MIQUELON

50F

MIQUELON - CHEVAUX EN LIBERTE

ACKNOWLEDGMENTS

We would like to thank the following individuals, companies, and institutions for permission to photograph and reproduce material from their collections, and for their invaluable help and advice: Friedl Expert Committee, New York; National Postal Museum, London; The Philatelic Foundation, New York, and especially Brian M. Green, assistant curator and Peter Robertson, curator; Alex Rendon, New York; Swiss PTT; Robert A. Siegel Auction Galleries, New York; Frank Warner, New York; Raymond H. Weill Co., New Orleans.

Our very special thanks go to Viola Ilma and to Richard E. Beresford, Director of Education, Philatelic Foundation.

Our thanks are also due to Steve Moore for all color photography, except that on pages 13, 34, 39, and to Carl Mammay for black-and-white and color photography.

Stamps in copyright are reproduced by courtesy of the British Post Office and the United States Postal Service.